COMMUNITY · CONNECTIONS

?

HOW DOES IT FLY?
HOT AIR BALLOON

BY NANCY ROBINSON MASTERS

Published in the United States of America by Cherry Lake Publishing
Ann Arbor, Michigan
www.cherrylakepublishing.com

Content Adviser: Jacob Zeiger, Production Support Engineer, the Boeing Company

Photo Credits: Cover and page 1, ©douglas knight/Shutterstock, Inc.; page 5, ©Manfred Steinbach/Shutterstock, Inc.; page 7, ©Steve Adamson/Shutterstock, Inc.; page 9, ©iStockphoto/duckycards; page 11, ©Jonathan Lenz/Shutterstock, Inc; page 13, ©afarland/Shutterstock, Inc.; page 15, ©italianestro/Shutterstock, Inc.; page 17, ©Oleg Kozlov/Shutterstock, Inc.; page 19, ©Michael Rolands/Dreamstime.com; page 21, ©Yoav Sinai/Dreamstime.com

LIBRARY OF CONGRESS CATALOGING-IN-PUBLICATION DATA
Masters, Nancy Robinson.
  How does it fly? Hot air balloon/by Nancy Robinson Masters.
    p. cm.—(Community connections)
  Includes bibliographical references and index.
  ISBN-13: 978-1-61080-068-6 (library binding)
  ISBN-10: 1-61080-068-0 (library binding)
  1. Hot air balloons—Juvenile literature. I. Title. II. Title: Hot air balloon. III. Series.
  TL638.M37 2012
  629.133'22—dc22   2011003310

Cherry Lake Publishing would like to acknowledge the work of The Partnership for 21st Century Skills. Please visit www.21stcenturyskills.org for more information.

Printed in the United States of America
Corporate Graphics Inc.
July 2011
CLFA09

CONTENTS

HOW DOES IT FLY?

WHAT IS A HOT AIR BALLOON?

A hot air balloon is a kind of aircraft. It has three main parts.

The **envelope** is the largest part. It is the colorful part that looks like a large balloon. The envelope is also called a bag. Huge pieces of strong **fabric** are sewn together to make the bag.

Have you ever seen a hot air balloon in flight?

The burner system is under the bag. The burner burns fuel to heat the air in the bag.

The basket carries the pilot and passengers. Some baskets can carry about 20 people. Most baskets are made of wicker fiber. Wicker fiber is made from plants.

The pilot uses the burner to heat the air in the bag during flight.

The most popular balloons are made in fun shapes. They often have bright colors.

Artists design pictures on some balloon bags. They draw their designs on paper first. They make sure the image will fit the shape and size of the balloon.

Bag fabric can be sewn in many different shapes and sizes.

8

Imagine you are a hot air balloon artist. Draw a picture you would paint on a balloon's bag. Remember to think big!

GETTING OFF THE GROUND

Calm winds are needed to **launch** a hot air balloon. **Chase crew** workers unpack the bag on flat ground. They check for tears in the fabric. They make sure the bag is correctly attached to the basket.

The pilot plans where to land the balloon. The **landing site** may be a field or park.

The empty bag is spread on the ground before it is hooked to the basket.

The bag is ready to **inflate**. The chase crew holds the bottom of the bag open. Fans blow air into the bag. The pilot uses the burner to heat the air.

The hot air causes the bag to stand up. Passengers climb into the basket. The filled bag lifts the basket off the ground.

12

The pilot and crew work together to inflate the balloon bag.

Balloon bags are made of fabric. If you were making a balloon bag, what properties would you want the fabric to have? Why?

13

STAYING UP

Flash! The burner sends a blast of heat into the bag. Cool air in the bag will not keep the balloon up.

The pilot is careful not to waste fuel. He does not want to use the burner too much. Too much heat can burn the fabric.

A passenger takes pictures after the pilot has turned off the burner.

15

The pilot does not have controls to steer the balloon. He uses the burner to make the balloon climb or **descend**. He climbs and descends to find wind that will blow the balloon toward the landing site.

The pilot must find a safe **altitude** at which to fly. This keeps the balloon from blowing into trees or other tall objects.

16

Pilots use maps and other instruments to help them know about they area they are flying over.

Hot air balloons depend on wind for movement. Which way will a balloon go if there is no wind blowing?

17

MAKING A LANDING

The chase crew follows the balloon to the landing site. The pilot and the crew use radios and telephones to talk with each other.

The pilot watches for the landing site. He stops using the burner to heat the air. The air in the balloon cools. The balloon descends.

A pilot descends to join other hot air balloons at a landing site.

The pilot pulls a rope attached to the top of the balloon. The top opens. The air goes out. The bag **deflates**.

The basket lands first. The bag falls to the ground. The pilot and chase crew pack up the bag. They check the burner and basket for any damage. The hot air balloon is then stored away, kept safe until the next launch!

A balloon needs to land in a space large enough for the bag to deflate safely.

Look around your neighborhood. Is there a safe place for a hot air balloon to land?

21

GLOSSARY

altitude (AL-ti-tood) distance above the ground

chase crew (CHASE KROO) workers who help a hot air balloon launch and land

deflates (di-FLATES) loses air

descend (di-SEND) go downward

envelope (EN-vuh-lope) large bag that holds hot air to make a hot air balloon float

fabric (FAB-rik) cloth

inflate (in-FLATE) fill with air

landing site (LAN-ding SITE) the location where a hot air balloon or other flying machine will land

launch (LAWNCH) send off

FIND OUT MORE

BOOKS

Hicks, Kelli L. *Hot Air Ballooning*. Vero Beach, FL: Rourke Publishing, 2010.

Rau, Dana Meachen. *Hot Air Balloons*. New York: Marshall Cavendish Benchmark, 2011.

WEB SITES

Cameron Balloons
www.cameronballoons.com/images.html
Look at photos of all kinds of hot air balloons.

National Balloon Museum
www.nationalballoonmuseum.com
Find information and take a look at exhibits about hot air balloons.

INDEX

24

ABOUT THE AUTHOR

Nancy Robinson Masters is an airplane pilot and the author of more than 40 books. She and her husband, Bill, live at an airport near Abilene, Texas. Bill is a hot air balloon pilot, and Nancy is part of his chase crew.